AUTHOR'S PREFACE

Monitors, especially Savannah Monitors, have seen an increase in popularity during recent years. The current interest in dinosaurs has no doubt contributed to this popularity and seeing a group of monitors in a large, well-decorated terrarium can indeed be like taking a glimpse into the age when the giant lizards were masters of the earth.

Monitors are lizards which form part of the reptilian order Squamata, sharing it with the snakes and the amphisbaenians. There are about forty species of monitor, including the largest of all living lizards, the Komodo Dragon, which can reach a length of 10 ft/3 m. While the Savannah Monitor does not reach that size (thank goodness for those herpetologists who live in small apartments), it can be said to possess all the attributes of these giant lizards in convenient and compact form.

I have had the good fortune to look after a good number of Savannah Monitors during my years as a reptile house curator in the 1970's and thus have a special affection for them. Since those days, the keeping of exotic pets in the home is becoming ever more popular. Because a great part of the population lives in towns and cities, and the concrete jungle is no substitute for the real thing, a large number of people tend to crave for some kind of substitute for the great outdoors and all of its creatures. In some people this manifests itself in the keeping of one or more exotic pets, and monitor lizards are included in the want lists of some such people.

The general human attitude toward th[...] animals creatures [...] than it ha[...] the past, [...] increasing[...] excellent wildlife

It is thought that the Savannah Monitor's, *Varanus exanthematicus*, dinosaur-like appearance has contributed greatly to its popularity in the herpetocultural hobby. Photo by R. D. Bartlett.

films we can see on television. Conservationists have also shown us the very real fear and realization that many exotic animals are on an irreversible decline in population, due largely to man's destruction, or alteration of the environment "for economic gain." Unfortunately we currently seem to be witnessing the most rapid demise of biological diversity in the history of life itself! The Savannah Monitor, like many reptiles, is threatened in many parts of its range due to loss of or change of habitat and, regrettably, exploitation for skins.

Responsible and caring attitudes toward our pet monitors will go a long way toward ensuring their survival in captivity at least. Savannah Monitors are special lizards that soon become tame and trusting, indeed almost affectionate. They are reasonably intelligent, have a relatively easy diet, and can be kept in a small apartment. With proper care they will not emit unpleasant odors and they are not noisy or in any way disruptive to your family or neighbors. Indeed, the latter need not even know you have them.

This small book has been prepared specially for those people who have a soft spot for Savannah Monitors. Those people who have an desire to own one, or preferably a pair, will find all they need here to keep them in the best of health and perhaps to breed them. Additionally, the book will hopefully be of some interest to the general naturalist who may like to learn   some more detail about these fascinating creatures.

John Coborn
Nanango, Queensland, Australia

The monitors, like so many other animals, are disappearing from the wild at an alarming rate. If you are capable of breeding your monitors, it is advised that you do so. Shown is a White-throated Monitor, *Varanus albigularis*.

K. H. SWITAK

MONITOR BIOLOGY AND CLASSIFICATION

REPTILES IN GENERAL

Being reptiles, Savannah Monitors have several recognizable characteristics that they share with all other reptiles. The most obvious are that they possess a scaly skin, respire by means of lungs, and are ectothermic or "cold-blooded" (relying on external warmth—sunlight—in order to maintain a comfortable body temperature). These three attributes separate reptiles from the other vertebrate classes, as no other class has all three of them.

temperature they return to a cooler spot until it is time to warm up again.

MONITORS IN GENERAL

Monitor lizards form the saurian family Varanidae, which contains about 40 species found from Africa through southern Asia and the Indo-Papuan region to Australia, where species are most numerous. All of the species are carnivorous and oviparous, and most are diurnal. The family includes the world's largest lizard, the Komodo Dragon, *Varanus*

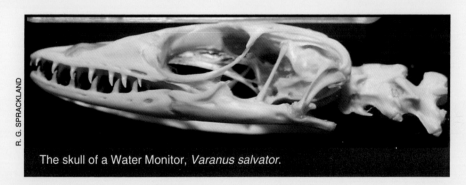

R. G. SPRACKLAND

The skull of a Water Monitor, *Varanus salvator*.

Being "cold-blooded," reptiles cannot maintain a constant average body temperature by metabolic means (as can birds and mammals), but they are able to regulate their temperatures to a certain extent by a process known as "thermoregulation." They do this by simply moving into a warmer spot (into the sun, or on, in, or under a sun-warmed object) when they feel too cold. When they reach a preferred

komodoensis, of Indonesia. Some of the more important diagnostic characteristics of monitors are as follows:

1. The elongated body and the head are usually covered with relatively small scales.
2. There are two pairs of powerful, well-developed limbs, and each limb is furnished with five strongly clawed digits.
3. The snout is typically long and

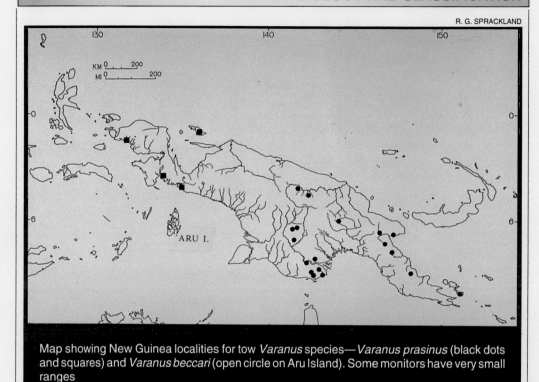

R. G. SPRACKLAND

Map showing New Guinea localities for tow *Varanus* species—*Varanus prasinus* (black dots and squares) and *Varanus beccari* (open circle on Aru Island). Some monitors have very small ranges

narrow, and the tail is very long and usually laterally flattened.

4. The large, sharp, usually pointed teeth are mounted on the sides of the jaws (pleurodontid).

5. The relatively long tongue is smooth, forked, retractile, and snake-like.

6. The efficient eyes are furnished with well-developed movable lids.

THE SAVANNAH MONITOR IN PARTICULAR

The Savannah Monitor, *Varanus exanthematicus*, occurs naturally in suitable habitats throughout Africa south of the Sahara. Scientists currently recognize five subspecies:

1. *Varanus exanthematicus* (Bosc, 1792); Senegal east to Ethiopia.

2. *V. e. albigularis* (Daudin, 1802): Namibia, Botswana, Republic of South Africa, Zimbabwe, Mozambique, and Zambia. (This is often recognized as a separate species by many taxonomists.)

3. *V. e. angolensis* Schmidt 1934: Angola.

4. *V. e. ionidesi* Laurent 1964: East Africa.

5. *V. e. microstictus* Boettger 1893: Mozambique.

The subspecies are generally similar in appearance and are separated only by small anatomical differences. Savannah Monitors are becoming scarce or even absent from many of their former haunts, probably due to over-collection for skins and loss

This artwork shows the comparative size differences between the Komodo Dragon, *Varanus komodoensis* (on the bottom), one normal-sized adult male, and five extinct reptiles. From the top, *Hainosaurus*, *Plotosaurus*, *Tyrannosaurus* (right), *Iguanodon* (left), and *Megalania*, this latter genus being an extinct giant monitor. Illustration by John R. Quinn.

of habitat from human encroachment. Within its immense geographical range, the Savannah Monitor occurs in a wide variety of habitats, from open woodland through savannah to semi-desert, but it tends to avoid heavily forested or wetter regions. It usually lives in areas where reasonable cover is available, such as among rocky outcrops, or thick, low vegetation, where it takes refuge in burrows or crevices, often beneath rocks or logs. Though it spends most of its time on the ground, it can climb if necessary and may often hunt for prey among tree branches. It is an adept swimmer when the situation arises and also likes to bathe for long periods when conditions permit.

It is a large, robustly built, and spectacular lizard. The maximum length is 5 ft/1.5 m, but the average is around 3 ft 3 in/1 m. More than half of the length is taken up by the laterally flattened tail. Maximum weight is about 10 lbs/5 kg, though obese captive

One of the smaller monitors, the Spotted Tree Monitor, *Varanus timorensis*, grows to only about two feet in length. It spends much of its time in trees and feeds on insects and smaller lizards.

PAUL FREED

K. H. SWITAK

The Spiny-tail Monitor, *Varanus acanthurus*, occurs over most of northern Australia and grows to a length of about 28 in/71 cm.

specimens may become even heavier. The body is flat-oval in section, and the head is relatively broad and the snout rounded in contrast to the narrow, pointed heads and snouts of most other monitors. The neck also is relatively short. The body and head are covered with relatively small, granular scales.

The ground color of the body typically is dull yellowish gray, broken with dark-edged lighter yellowish patches and a scattering of paler scales. The underside generally is uniformly pale. Juvenile specimens usually are somewhat brighter in color with a greater contrast in the pattern. The sexes are very similar, but males can be distinguished from the females by their generally larger size and by the presence of two lateral bulges at the base of the tail, each of which contains a hemipenis, half of the male's copulatory organ. The male's head also is more robust than that of the female.

The long tail is used as a balancing aid during the lizard's normal activities and, although not prehensile, the tail can be used as a steadying or thrusting aid to locomotion in various circumstances. The tail may also be used as a weapon of defense, being lashed in a whiplike fashion and aimed at a potential adversary. If cornered or seized, the Savannah Monitor uses not only its tail in defense—its pointed claws are capable of ripping into the human skin, and its sharp, serrate rows of teeth also should be treated with respect. Thankfully, such brusque defensive behavior is soon lost by captive specimens, which can usually be handled with reasonable safety once they are accustomed to your attention, though you should always be wary of accidental scratching from the claws!

Savannah Monitors are preyed upon by a variety of animals in their native habitats. Large African pythons will prey upon adult monitors, while the juveniles are preyed upon by smaller snake species. Birds of prey and carnivorous mammals, including big cats, hyenas, wild dogs, and so on find monitors delicious. Native Africans have also included monitor on their menus for generations. All of these predators have little impact on populations of monitors as they are all part of the natural ecology.

The impact of modern society on the African continent, however, has spelled disaster for Savannah Monitors as well as for many other animal species. In some areas, human populations have increased a thousandfold, with the resulting losses of habitats. Living and breeding sites for monitors have been replaced by housing developments, mines, factories, and agricultural areas. The natives still continue to eat the monitors that are left, but to make matters worse, the lucrative international trade in lizard skins is still a major factor in the demise of these delightful lizards. In 1981, for example, 240,000 Savannah

Only described as a full species in 1980, the Argus Monitor, *Varanus panoptes*, spends much of its time near waterways, where it feeds mostly on aquatic prey items.

Monitor skins were exported, mostly from Nigeria and Sudan, and the countries that imported most of these were Germany, Italy and the USA. Though numbers of exports have diminished since then, this probably reflects more on the availability of surviving numbers than the enthusiasm of the exporters and importers!

The efforts of conservationists in recent years have persuaded the governments of many

PAUL FREED

utmost importance. If species become even more endangered, as they inevitably will with the way things are going, the breeding of captive stock will be the only way to produce further specimens for enthusiasts.

CLASSIFICATION

Being lizards, Savannah Monitors are classified in the suborder Sauria. Within the Sauria there are 19 families of lizards with over 3000 species. The Savannah Monitor and all of its 40 or so relatives are placed together in the family Varanidae. As varanids all have very much in common with each other they are all placed in a single genus *Varanus*.

For the present, the following table shows how *Varanus exanthematicus* fits into the animal kingdom:

countries to see the importance of preserving their varieties of wildlife, and Savannah Monitors, like all *Varanus* species, are listed in the appendices of the Convention on International Trade in Endangered Species of Wild Flora and Fauna (CITES), which means that international trade of the species is only allowed under special license, and even then there are strict regulations with regard to the capture, restraint, husbandry, and transport of specimens. All of this is, of course, a big reason why captive-breeding of our reptiles is of

Kingdom: Animalia. All animals
Phylum: Chordata. Animals with notochord
Subphylum: Vertebrata. Backboned animals
Class: Reptilia. All reptiles
Order: Squamata. All lizards and snakes
Suborder: Sauria. All lizards
Family: Varanidae. All monitor lizards
Genus: *Varanus.* Monitor Lizards
Subgenus: *Polydaedalus.* Savannah Monitors
Species: *V. exanthematicus.* Savannah Monitor

J. VISSER

The Savannah Monitor, *Varanus exanthematicus*, above, is probably kept more often than any of the other varanids. Conversely, the Komodo Dragon, *Varanus komodoensis*, below, is perhaps the most legendary and least-seen in captivity. It wasn't described until 1912, after a report made by a Dutch pilot who claimed to have been marooned on an island inhabited by "dragons."

JOHN COBORN

HOUSING SAVANNAH MONITORS

Accommodations for captive reptiles are varied; there are no hard and fast rules as long as the necessary life-support systems are present (heating, lighting, ventilation, etc.). Additionally, cages should be 1) of sufficient size to house the animals in question, 2) easy to clean and service, 3) escape-proof, and 4) should have an attractive appearance. A cage in which reptiles are kept is often referred to as a vivarium or terrarium, the latter meaning "enclosed landscape," distinct from the "enclosed waterscape" of an aquarium.

As long as the parameters mentioned above are taken into consideration, the shape of a terrarium is immaterial. You could buy a terrarium complete with all its life-support systems already intact, but many enthusiasts still prefer to make their own. These can be constructed from various materials and it is interesting to experiment with odds and ends you may obtain from second-hand or do-it-yourself stores.

Glass aquarium tanks have their uses, especially for juvenile monitor lizards. A couple of young monitors to 12 in/ 30 cm in length will live comfortably in a glass tank 24 x 12 x 12 in/60 x 30 x 30 cm, but must be moved to more voluminous accommodations as they increase in size.

It is possible to construct glass terrariums in many shapes and sizes by using silicone adhesive to cement the edges of the glass together. If you use a combination of glass and acrylic materials, you can have ventilation holes drilled in the sides or back (it is easy to drill holes in acrylic sheeting). The terrarium lid is preferably made of plywood or plastic, forming a shallow, box-like cavity into which the heating and lighting

Using full-spectrum lights simulates the natural environment of your Savannah Monitor. Photo courtesy of Coralife/Energy Savers.

R. G. SPRACKLAND

Wood and cork products are acceptable for use with monitors, but the keeper must remember that such products can be very difficult to clean. Species shown is an Emerald Tree Monitor, *Varanus prasinus*.

apparatus can be concealed from view from the outside. It is best to cover the electrical apparatus with wire mesh so that the inmates cannot gain access to it and electrocute or burn themselves. The minimum size a tank should be for a couple of juvenile monitors (up to one year old) is about 2 cubic feet/0.17 cubic meters.

Timber is a good material for terrarium construction but the wood must have a few coats of varnish or non-toxic paint to prevent it from deteriorating in damp or very dry conditions. A simple terrarium, for juvenile monitors, consisting of a plywood box with a framed glass front is easy to make. Using 0.5 in/10 mm plywood, the top, bottom, and ends are simply glued and tacked together. A terrarium with dimensions 3 ft x 18 in x 18 in/ 90 cm x 45 cm x 45 cm is adequate for a pair of young Savannah Monitors up to about 18 in/45 cm in length.

Though you can make such a cage from new timber, I have seen many fine terraria manufactured from such things as old wardrobes or chests of drawers, from which the insides and doors

for your Savannah Monitors with concrete blocks or bricks. This could include a drainable concrete pool and artificial cliff-faces with ledges. Such a permanent terrarium, built into a part of the house or apartment, could be an attractive feature and a focal point in the den, living room, hall, or conservatory. The terrarium can be free standing or you might want to use an existing alcove somewhere in your house. A visit to a zoological park that has a reptile display

Gravel makes an ideal substrate for many reasons. First, it is washable and therefore reusable. Also, it can be purchased at most pet shops and in a variety of sizes and colors. Photo of a Spiny-tail Monitor, (*Varanus acanthurus*), by William B. Allen, Jr.

have been removed. You may be able to get some old aluminum or timber framed windows from a demolition yard and incorporate these in your terrarium. The minimum dimensions for a pair of adults should be 6 ft x 6 ft x 3 ft/ 180 cm x 180 cm x 90 cm.

THE PERMANENT TERRARIUM

You can build a very substantial and permanent cage

will be likely to give you several ideas for inclusion in your home terrarium.

Before commencing any major construction, however, be sure you are not violating any local building or construction regulations. It may also be a good idea to get engineering or plumbing advice before introducing weighty structures into your home.

TERRARIUM FURNISHINGS AND DECORATIONS

Your monitor cages will require various furnishings which are both functional and decorative. Although it is possible to keep the lizards in almost "clinical" conditions (a sheet of absorbent paper, a waterbowl, and a place to hide), most enthusiasts want a terrarium that is a decorative feature in their home. However, the clinical method can still be convenient if you want to keep several breeding pairs or colonies.

Floor Coverings: These are many and varied but it is perhaps best to use washed gravel which can be obtained in various grades (pea-sized shingle is perhaps the ideal size for monitors). Do not use very fine sand, as it tends to cake between the reptiles's scales. Some enthusiasts like to use paper towels or artificial grass. Whatever substrate material you use, it must be removed and washed, or replaced, at regular intervals.

Rocks: These come in an enormous range of interesting shapes and sizes. They are not only decorative in the terrarium, but can also be used as basking sites, hiding places, to help to keep a monitor's nails trim, and to increase the area of exercise available to your pets. You may

A leafy, sandy substrate will give any monitor enclosure a natural and visually attractive feel. Species shown is a New Guinea Crocodile Monitor, *Varanus salvadori*.

R. D. BARTLETT

R. G. SPRACKLAND

This Mangrove Monitor, *Varanus indicus*, is standing on a substrate of wood shavings, which are very commonly used in the herpetocultural hobby. Beware, however, of shavings of the cedar variety, for the oils contained therein cause reptiles to develop skin problems.

be able to get suitable rocks at your local pet store or garden center, but it is much more exciting to go out on location and find your own (make sure you have permission to take rocks away from private land). Always ensure that rocks are placed firmly so they cannot fall down and injure the reptiles. If you are using large piles of rocks, it is best to cement them together to prevent accidents.

Logs and Branches: A strong tree branch will be used by monitors to climb and gain additional exercise. It is more practical to use dead tree branches rather than to try and grow trees or shrubs in the terrarium unless the accommodation is very voluminous. Look for branches with interesting shapes; gnarled and twisted limbs are always attractive to look at. Driftwood collected from the sea shore or from river banks is often esthetically pleasing as it will have been weathered by the sand, sun, and water. Hollow logs are very useful as they provide natural refuges for the monitors. All wood should be scrubbed thoroughly and then rinsed and dried before being used.

Plants: Vibrant, living plants in the terrarium doubtlessly provide a subtle esthetic touch. However,

Putting a scenic sheet onto the back of your monitor's tank like the one on the back of this bearded dragon's tank, will greatly enhance the setup's visual effect. Such sheets can be purchased at most pet shops and come in a variety of tableaux.

A sheet of artificial turf makes a great bedding for a Savannah Monitor's enclosure. Such sheets can be purchased, pre-cut to fit most aquariums, at many herp-oriented pet shops. Photo courtesy of Four Paws.

unless the terrarium is very large, it is futile to try and grow plants where large robust monitors are being kept, as the plants will be continually uprooted or flattened. We will therefore have to compromise with robust, plastic artificial plants (fortunately, some quite realistic types are now available) or make do without plants. A couple of robust potted plants could probably be placed in a terrarium with juvenile monitors, but the earth in the pots should be protected with large pebbles to prevent uprooting. Choose plant species compatible to the type of environment in the terrarium. Many so-called house plants are suitable. It will be useful for you to study a good book on plant culture to aid in your selection.

TERRARIUM HEATING

Like all reptiles, monitors are cold-blooded, or

poikilothermic. This means that they maintain their body temperature by moving in and out of warm places, i.e., by basking directly in the sun or absorbing heat from sun-warmed soil, rocks, or other items.

Unless you are lucky enough to live in the tropics, you will need supplementary heating in your terrarium. Using natural sunlight through terrarium glass poses problems of overheating, though this can be overcome in the summer by using insect screening or mesh instead of glass. At other times, artificial means of heating have to be employed.

Remember that Savannah Monitors require a substantial reduction in temperature at night. In the home, this can be accomplished by simply switching off the heat source and allowing the terrarium to cool to room temperature, as long as this does not drop below 54°F/12°C. You should aim to maintain daytime temperatures between 82 and 95°F/28 and 35°C, reducing this to about 60 to 68°F/16 to 20°C at night.

A number of different heating devices can be used. Ordinary household incandescent light bulbs had long been used as a sole source of heating and lighting in the home terrarium until it was discovered that the quality of light emitted was insufficient for diurnal basking lizards. Incandescent bulbs should not be ignored altogether, however, as they are inexpensive, emit a fair amount of heat, and are a supplementary source of light. The internal dimensions of the terrarium will dictate what size bulb(s) to use. By experimenting with various wattages and a thermometer, suitable temperatures will be arrived at. A light bulb can be concealed inside a metal canister and controlled by a thermostat so that a constant, minimum background temperature is maintained.

Heating-lamps of various kinds are available. Some, of the type used in poultry brooders or

Heat is, of course, an essential provision for captive monitors. Heated stones have become very popular in the herpetocultural hobby and are available at most pet shops that stock other herp-oriented products. Photo courtesy of Zoo Med.

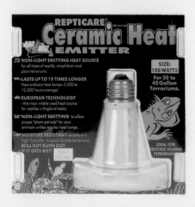

"Spot heating" is one effective way to provide a monitor with bodily warmth. Ceramic emitters direct heat to a single spot in an enclosure, where a monitor can then either lay or leave when it wishes. Photo courtesy of Zoo Med.

piggeries, produce infra-red or white radiant heat. Such lamps are very useful for directing at basking areas. A heat lamp should be installed at one end only, thus creating a temperature gradation from one end of the cage to the other. Your monitors will then be able to seek out their own preferred temperatures. Ceramic heating plates or bulbs are also available. Sometimes referred to as "black light" bulbs, these emit heat but no light and are useful for maintaining background heat at night.

Cable heaters and pads of the type used by horticulturists in their propagating boxes can be used for heating parts of the substrate. They are good for background heat or in the provision of additional basking areas.

Aquarium heaters are useful for maintaining warmth plus

humidity in the terrarium and are useful during your simulated "wet season." Placed in the water body, an aquarium heater will keep the water warm and the air warm and humid. By using an aquarium aerator pump as well you will further increase humidity, help raise the air temperature, provide additional ventilation, and help keep the water fresh.

Under-tank heating pads are inexpensive, come in a variety of sizes and wattages, and are a very sensible way to provide a monitor with bodily warmth. These pads can be found at most pet shops. Photo courtesy of Zoo Med.

TERRARIUM LIGHTING

Natural sunlight or a good substitute is very important for maintaining good health in Savannah Monitors. The most important constituents of sunlight are the ultraviolet rays that help stimulate the manufacture of vitamin D3 in the reptilian skin. This vitamin is essential for controlling the action of the important minerals calcium and

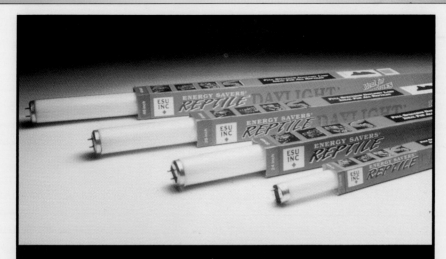

The accurate replication of photoperiods is essential to good Savannah Monitor husbandry. Your local pet shop should carry the bulbs that will suit your pets' needs. Photo courtesy of Coralife/Energy Savers.

phosphorus in the body; without it, various health problems will ensue. By all means, allow your monitors to have unfiltered natural sunlight, if possible, by allowing it to pass through mesh.

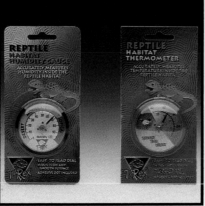

It is always a good idea to keep an eye on your monitor's ambient temperature. There are a number of thermometers that can, and should, be used with reptile setups. Photo courtesy of Ocean Nutrition.

Natural sunlight through glass is of little value as much of the benefit of the ultraviolet rays is lost. In temperate areas it is impossible to place terraria outside for most of the year, so compromise lighting of good quality must be provided. Special fluorescent tubes which emit a preponderance of light from the "blue" end of the spectrum will provide sufficient ultraviolet light for your monitors. Be aware, however, that too much ultraviolet light can be more damaging than too little. Research into suitable light sources for horticulture, aquariums, and terrariums is continuing, and information on suitable systems may be obtained from aquarist's suppliers or manufacturers.

HUMIDITY

Savannah Monitors require fairly low humidity for most of the year, but a simulated wet-season, with increased humidity, will not go amiss and may trigger a breeding response. As most kinds of heating apparatus in the terrarium tend to create a dry atmosphere, you will have no problems for most of the year. When you require an increase in humidity, however, it will be necessary to use additional apparatus. An aquarium heater used in the water bath will help, and, as mentioned above, an aerator used in the water will further increase the humidity and air temperature. The simplest method of maintaining humidity in a cage, of course, is to mist-spray, but this may have to be done several times a day.

VENTILATION

Within the close confines of the terrarium adequate ventilation is essential. Poor ventilation will lead to a build up of stale air and an excess of carbon dioxide, providing favorable conditions for disease organisms to thrive and multiply as well as causing stress in your animals and a resulting reduced resistance to disease. A constant air exchange in the terrarium must be arranged, but without creating excessive cold drafts. In most cases, the provision of

adequate ventilation holes in the sides and top of a terrarium is all that is required; the warmth generated by the heating apparatus will cause air convection currents, the warm air leaving through the top and fresh air replacing it through the side vents.

ROOM TERRARIUMS

A very satisfactory method of keeping Savannah Monitors is to turn a whole room over to them. You can only create a room terrarium, of course, if you have a suitable spare room and the facilities to heat it. Central heating radiators and pipes are ideal for background heating, and you can install one or two heat lamps over basking spots. All heating apparatus must be screened with mesh to prevent the lizards gaining contact with it and getting burned.

In the summer you can open windows for fresh air, ventilation, and perhaps some unfiltered sunlight. Needless to say, the windows should be covered with strong mesh screens to prevent escapes. A large water bath is essential, and, since monitors drink often as well as bathe, it is important the water is replaced as frequently as possible.

Bark nuggets make a good bedding for Savannah Monitors. They can be purchased at most pet shops in either small bags or bulk quantities. Photo courtesy of Four Paws.

R. G. SPRACKLAND

If you can spare it, you might want to consider giving your monitor a whole room all to itself. The best rooms in a house to do this in are those that aren't considered "major," i.e., those in the attic, cellar, etc. Species shown is a Savannah Monitor, *Varanus exanthematicus*.

The lizards should also be given rocks and climbing logs, fixed securely so that they cannot fall over and cause accidents.

Keeping a monitor outside is obviously the best way to provide it with things like sunlight and good ventiliation. Although most keepers find the task of building an outdoor enclosure very time-consuming and costly, the results can be most rewarding. Species shown is a Nile Monitor, *Varanus niloticus*.

K. H. SWITAK

R. G. SPRACKLAND

You will find that most monitors are very willing and eager feeders, like this Water Monitor, *Varanus salvator*, obviously is, but be careful when offering food by hand—the monitor might want the hand too!

FEEDING SAVANNAH MONITORS

All animals require a balanced diet in order to function successfully. In the wild, animal species obtain their balanced diet requirements by feeding upon the type and variety of food items available in their natural habitats. Bear in mind that a species will have evolved in that habitat through millions of years and there will therefore be a very close relationship between it and the food available. However, these different species not only acquire these dietary constituents in different ways, they may require them in varied percentages as well.

The wild diet of lizards is studied mainly by identifying prey in the stomach contents. This may be done by examining the stomach contents of dead, preserved specimens, or, more humanely, to flush out the stomachs of live lizards to remove what has been eaten. Diet studies on many *Varanus* species have shown them to be almost wholly carnivorous (one species, *Varanus olivaceous*, is the only monitor known to deliberately consume vegetable matter). Juvenile Savannah Monitors feed largely upon invertebrates (snails, slugs, earthworms, grasshoppers, cockroaches, beetles, and so on) but as they mature they take progressively larger amounts of amphibian, reptile, bird, and mammal meat. Food may be captured live or carrion may be eaten. Only food items of a size that can be swallowed whole are usually taken.

Savannah Monitors use the typical varanid means of hunting for food. They walk with their characteristic swinging gait with the snout held close to the substrate. The long forked, tongue flickers constantly, picking up scent particles to locate prey even when it is below the surface. The tips of the forked tongue correspond with a pair of sensory organs in the palate which correspond with the nostrils, but are separate from them. These organs, called

B. KAHL

Being largely carnivorous, monitors will gladly take mice of any size. This Gould's Monitor, *Varanus gouldi*, for example, seems perfectly content with the pinkie mouse it has acquired.

Jacobson's organs, are particularly sensitive in snakes and in many lizards, including monitors. Once scent has been located and passed into the organs via the tongue, a message to the brain tells the monitor what food is about. Then they use their strong limbs and claws, as well as the snout, for digging the prey out.

The dietary requirements of captive reptiles have recently been the subject of fairly concentrated studies in the scientific community, especially since veterinarians are turning their attentions to the more exotic household pets. Previously, diets were mainly speculative, based on our knowledge of what the particular species was known to eat in the wild coupled with what we knew about the nutritional husbandry of domestic or agricultural animals.

Many pet lizards perished as a result of some form of nutritional disturbance, largely through some ignorance on the part of their owners. We are now, however, at the happy stage where no captive monitor need die through ignorance; the means of keeping them alive, happy, and healthy are available, so be sure you are aware of the necessary information.

A primary consideration regarding the captive diet of Savannah Monitors is that it is a variety of food items that ensures the balanced diet. Even with a great variety of foods it is still considered necessary to provide additional vitamin/mineral supplements.

It has to be assumed that the variety of foods taken by wild lizards will constitute a balanced diet. The young are largely insectivorous during their early period of growth, feeding on a variety of invertebrates, then begin to take small vertebrates as they grow. The invertebrate food is important in providing adequate proteins, vitamins, and minerals during the critical early period of growth.

K. H. SWITAK

Since monitors are such enthusiastic feeders, it is strongly advised that you give them as many different items as they are willing to accept. This Savannah Monitor, *Varanus exanthematicus*, for example, will probably accept mice, crickets, raw beef, and perhaps even chicks.

FOOD ITEMS

One of the attractions of keeping Savannah Monitors is that they are relatively simple to feed. Young specimens can be reared on a variety of insects, including mealworms, grasshoppers, and crickets. Some of these insects are now commercially available and can be purchased in regular small amounts. You may want to breed your own insects, in which case crickets and mealworms are probably the easiest. Additionally, they may be given the occasional meal of minced lean beef or ox-heart, which can be fortified with a raw egg. Canned cat food or dog food may be given, although sparingly since it is likely to be too rich and fattening. Your feeding strategy may be a matter of trial and error.

A multi-vitamin/mineral supplement powder should be sprinkled over the food regularly, especially if you are giving raw meat which may be low in vitamin and mineral content. Raw meat on its own is, in any case, inadequate and should be used only as a supplement to other foods. By far the best foods for medium-sized to adult monitors are mice, small rats, and young chickens, all of which may be given dead and whole. As long as these food animals have themselves been reared on a healthy diet, they will be an excellent food supply for your lizards. The advantage of whole food animals is that they contain all of the roughage of bone, fur and feather, as well as enough

R. G. SPRACKLAND

In zoos and other institutions where Komodo Dragons, *Varanus komodoensis*, are allowed to be kept, the food offerings are sometimes goats and pigs, the latter of which has been offered here. Of course, such food items are virtually impossible for most keepers to supply.

variety of main nutrients, minerals, and vitamins to supply a balanced diet.

With regard to quantities of food, that is another matter of trial and error. It is best to leave your monitors a little hungry rather than overfed. Since monitors are rather gluttonous, they will tend to eat more than is good for them if given the chance. Obese captive monitors, unfortunately, are common, tend to become infertile, and will probably die at an early age.

Some of the live foods suitable for the raising of juvenile Savannah Monitors are as follows:

Collected Live Foods: If you have a large garden, live in the country, or have regular access to the country, you can collect a variety of invertebrate foods for your monitors during the warmer parts of the year, then concentrate on cultivated foods in the winter. Such items as garden snails, large earthworms, and grasshoppers will usually be taken quite eagerly. Care should be taken not to use items that may have been contaminated with insecticides or other chemicals. Collected vertebrates (mice, rats etc.) are best avoided due to the possibility of transmission of parasites or diseases.

Propagated Foods: In addition to collected foods, there will be times when we must rely on cultivated live foods for our plastic trash can with great success, having cut out a hole in the lid and covered this with plastic sunscreening for ventilation purposes). Give the

PAUL FREED

Monitors will rarely turn their noses up at grasshoppers. Grasshoppers of any kind will make perfectly acceptable meals, but some keepers may find it difficult to track down someone who sells them.

monitors. The following is a selection of the types of live foods that are commonly propagated, available commercially and easy to breed at home if you wish:

Crickets: Crickets are a highly nutritious food item, and could be the most important item, for your juvenile monitors during the winter months. They are now cultured widely and are usually readily available from pet shops or by mail order. One of the most commonly cultured species is the domestic cricket, *Acheta domestica*. The crickets can be kept in any suitably sized, escape-proof container (I have used a crickets balls of bunched-up newspaper in which to hide. A small saucer containing a piece of wet cotton wadding or clean bath-sponge will provide drinking water for the insects. They can be fed on cereals and greenfood (grass, lettuce, cabbage, spinach, various fruits etc.). The adult crickets like to lay their eggs in a damp medium so provide a dish or two of moist sand or vermiculite. The dish should be removed to a separate container at regular intervals and replaced with a new one. If kept at a temperature of about 77°F/25°C, the eggs will hatch in about three weeks.

Many keepers prefer to give their monitor frozen-and-thawed mice rather than live mice. Such mice are now available in packages at your local pet shop. Photo courtesy of Ocean Nutrition.

Grasshoppers: One species of grasshopper, the migratory locust, *Locusta migratoria*, is also often available from specialist suppliers and can be obtained in various instar sizes ranging from about .25 in/5 mm to the adult size of 2 in/5 cm. Adult locusts are excellent food for juvenile Savannah Monitors, and may even be accepted by the adult lizards. They are a little more difficult to breed than crickets though any problems can be quickly overcome. They can be fed on a mixture of bran and crushed oats, supplemented by fresh greenfoods. Grass is a convenient greenfood which can be kept fresh by placing the stems in a bottle of water with wadding packed around the neck to prevent the insects falling in and drowning. Locusts are best kept at a temperature of about 82°F/28°C in a tall, well-ventilated aquarium tank or a glass fronted box. The eggs are laid in slightly damp sand to a depth of 1 in/2.5 cm.

Mealworms: These are the larval form of a type of flour beetle (*Tenebrio molitor*) and are one of the easiest food insects to

Mealworms, when used in conjunction with other meaty foods, will make an excellent addition to the Savannah Monitor diet. Photo courtesy of Fluker Farms.

propagate. Large mealworms are of a size suitable for hatchling monitors, though as a food item they are low in digestible calcium, so that should be used only as part of a more varied diet. In any case, they are best sprinkled with a little vitamin/mineral powder before being used.

A breeding colony can be set up with about 100 mealworms placed in a large plastic tray or box with a 2 in/5 cm layer of a 50/50 mixture of chicken meal and bran in the base. Cover with a piece of material or absorbent paper, on which a few slices of carrot or potato should be placed to provide moisture. The mealworms will eventually pupate, emerging a few weeks later as adult beetles. These will mate and lay eggs, starting your next generation of mealworms. For a sustainable supply of mealworms, maintain four cultures, starting a new one and discarding the oldest one each month.

Mice and Rats: Most Savannah Monitors will feed eagerly on mice or rats of various sizes. The availability of laboratory mice and rats makes these animals an almost staple diet for many captive reptiles. Reared on a balanced diet, these rodents themselves are a balanced diet for our lizards. Newborn mice (often known as "pinkies") are a useful food for hatchling monitors, and mice at various stages of growth are suitable for your monitors as they increase in size. Larger monitors will take small to full-grown rats depending on their size. A self-sufficient colony of rats and/or mice is quite easy to maintain but somewhat time consuming. If you do not want to take the trouble to do this, mice and rats can be purchased when needed from laboratories or specialist suppliers; the latter may even supply them in dead, deep-frozen form which can be fed to the reptiles after being thoroughly thawed out.

Chickens: The young chicks of domestic fowl may be obtained inexpensively from hatcheries either alive or dead (sometimes deep-frozen, or you can deep freeze them yourself). Chicks which have started to grow and are a few days old are more nutritious than hatchlings.

Various specialized products, designed specifically for use with reptiles, are available to aid in keeping healthy Savannah Monitors. Photo courtesy of Coralife/Energy Savers.

R. D. BARTLETT

Lizards seem particulary susceptible to nutritional deficiencies and thus the need for a varied diet is so strong. A monitor that is fed on only one item will develop many health problems in the long run, some of which may be irreversible. Species shown is a Golden Monitor, *Varanus flavescens*.

GENERAL CARE

Any animal kept in captivity is totally dependent on us for its welfare. Wild animals can at least seek out the conditions most favorable to them, and forage for their own food and water. In a cage or terrarium we must provide all of these items in sufficient degree or quantity. Such tasks are sure to take up a fair amount of your spare time and, unless you are absolutely certain your

up with a lizard about 5 ft/1.5 m long, which will require a large cage and will need to be taken out regularly for exercise. All of these points should first be considered.

SELECTING YOUR SAVANNAH MONITORS

Once you have made the decision to keep Savannah Monitors, be sure you have their accommodations arranged before

It is important that a keeper of monitors reazlizes that his or her pets are totally dependent on them for all their living requirements. This can be a very demanding responsibility and should be seriously considered before even making a purchase. Species shown is a Savannah Monitor, *Varanus exanthematicus*.

DAVID R. MOENICH

enthusiasm for keeping monitors is not going to wane, you should never acquire any in the first place.

Remember also that most Savannah Monitor pets are acquired as juveniles. As they are colorful, and cute looking, it is easy to buy them impulse. You should also bear in mind that if you rear just one of these juveniles successfully, you are going to end

you actually bring the reptiles home.

Since captive-breeding is such a rave these days, many of the specimens you find for sale will have been bred in captivity. This is good because these specimens will already be accustomed to captivity. They are also more likely to be healthy and to be feeding normally. You may even get to know their history, however brief this may be. Another good aspect of a captive-bred specimen— whether it has been bred in your country or captive-bred in and later exported from its home country—is that it means that one fewer has been collected from the

very important to ensure that you get healthy livestock at the outset.

Before purchasing a monitor, always check its health by giving it a thorough inspection. Look for signs of mites or ticks on the skin; these parasites can transport

R. D. BARTLETT

If you are not familiar enough with monitor biology to give your pet(s) an effective health check (at least once every month or two), then bring the animal(s) to a vet. It is important that all developing diseases be identified as early on as possible. Species shown is Merten's Monitor, *Varanus mertensi*.

wild.

More important than where your monitor comes from and whether it is captive-bred or wild-caught is the question of its health. Monitors are not the most expensive of reptiles, but they are far from the cheapest. Also, cost is only one consideration; there are many other reasons for avoiding the purchase of sick monitors. It is

blood-pathogenic organisms from one reptile to the next. A good dealer will, of course, have ensured that such pests have been eradicated before he or she offers the reptiles for sale. A mite-infested terrarium in a dealer's premises is an invitation to take your business elsewhere! Choose only those monitors with a clean, unbroken skin, (small, well-healed wound scars are fairly common on larger monitors and are usually no cause for concern) with no lumps, cysts, sores, or skin infections, and ensure that the reptile is clear-eyed, alert, and plump. Look for broken claws or damage to the tail. Examine the nose, mouth, and the vent for any signs of discharges that could

then being placed loose in boxes so that in the case of panicking through fear, they cannot run against the sides of the crates and damage their snouts, etc. Each reptile is preferably placed on its own in a separate bag, and a number of bags can be placed in a transport box. With larger lizards, ensure that each individual has

R. G. SPRACKLAND

The mortality rate among young lizards is particularly high, even with careful captive care, so you should be meticulous in your husbandry when keeping young monitors of any kind. Once they are about three or four years of age (and in good shape), they then can be considered reliably hardy. Species shown is a young Savannah Monitor, *Varanus exanthematicus*.

indicate disease or abnormality. Find out what the reptile had been feeding on; it is important to continue with a similar diet for a while at least until it is settled in. Then you can gradually acquaint it with a more varied diet if necessary.

TRANSPORTATION

Lizards are normally transported in cloth bags rather

its own compartment. Try to avoid transporting your reptiles during colder periods, otherwise arrange for some kind of temporary heating and/or insulation (styrofoam containers or liners are ideal). The monitors should reach their destination and be housed appropriately as soon as possible. If you are transporting a monitor from its place of purchase to your home, it is quite okay just to carry

it in its bag as long as the weather is not too cold and as long as the journey is a short one. For obvious reasons, you should never leave a reptile in a cold car overnight, nor should you leave one in a car in the hot sun.

QUARANTINE

In order to avoid the risk of introducing diseases to any existing stock you may have, new arrivals should always be subjected to a period of quarantine. If, after 21 days in isolation, the reptile is still healthy, you can reasonably assume it is safe to introduce to other stock. Other than the usual life-support systems, there is no need for any special decorations in the quarantine cage; keep it as simple as possible, and preferably in a separate room away from your other pets.

Robert G. Sprackland (facing page, the one wearing the hat) is well-known among monitor enthusiasts as one of the foremost experts on monitor history and care. His superb book *Giant Lizards* (above, also published by TFH), is considered a landmark work on the larger members of the suborder Sauria. It is a beautifully illustrated and intelligently written volume and contains a great deal of information on the family Varanidae.

HANDLING YOUR MONITORS

Handling techniques will depend on the age and size of the animal, but most Savannah Monitors become relatively easy to deal with once they are accustomed to regular handling. A juvenile monitor can be simply picked up with the hand around the body, holding it firmly but gently. Once used to being handled, the monitor will usually be quite happy to sit on your arm or shoulder, even when it grows to adult size. However, large untamed monitors should be treated with great respect and caution, as they not only have a powerful bite, they also have sharp claws and a powerful whiplike tail as well. Such large monitors are best restrained by gripping the neck firmly with one hand and extending the fingers to secure the front limbs, while the rear limbs are restrained with the other hand, with the tail tucked under the elbow.

CLEANING

To reduce the risk of disease outbreaks, the terrarium should not only have all the necessary life-support systems, must also be maintained in a scrupulously clean condition. Try, however, to develop a routine in which the animals are not stressed by over-disturbance. In the simplest type of terrarium (ideal for quarantine, hospitalization, rearing juveniles, etc.) absorbent paper towels may be used as a substrate, and this can easily be changed each time it becomes soiled. With other forms

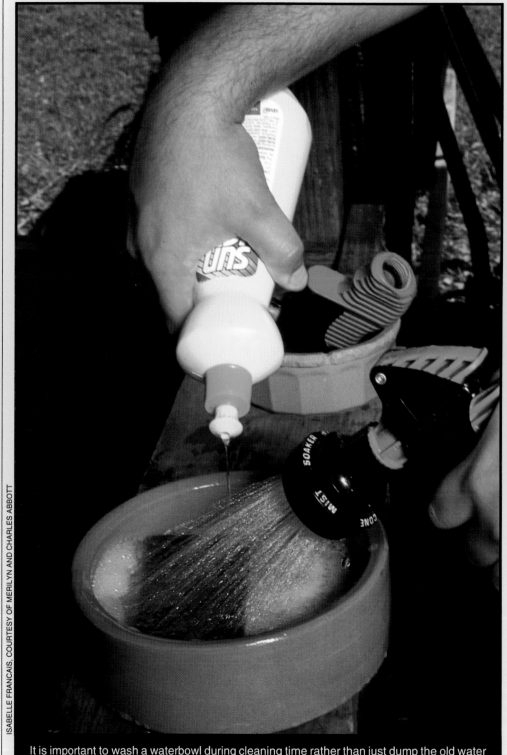

It is important to wash a waterbowl during cleaning time rather than just dump the old water out and add in the new. There are countless germs that find their way to a monitor's waterbowl, and thus vigorously cleaning the bowl is crucial.

Scrub a tank firmly and meticulously, but not with any abrasive materials; scratched glass looks awful! The scrub pad being used here is acceptble for the task as long as it is applied gently. Furthermore, keep in mind that scrub pads of any kind should only be used on really stubborn, dried-on filth. Beyond that, only soft sponges should be used.

JEFF BOUNDY

Above: It cannot be stressed enough that prompt cleaning of all feces should be executed habitually. Feces that are allowed to sit in a monitor's tank will cause disease organisms to spread like mad, creating a multitude of further problems in a very short time. Species shown is a Perentie, *Varanus giganteus*. **Below:** The proper place to grasp any monitor whose temperament you are unsusre of is just behind the head. The correct approach is accurately demonstrated in this photo. Species shown is a Water Monitor, *Varanus salvator*.

R. G. SPRACKLAND AND GARY GYAKI

of substrate, such as sand or gravel, the droppings must be removed daily using a scoop or small shovel. Unless suffering from diarrhea, monitor droppings are fairly solid and easy to pick up, especially if the monitors are fed regularly on whole prey animals. About once per month

bleach or povidone-iodine, then thoroughly swilled out with clean water before being dried and refurnished.

During cleaning operations the reptiles can be placed in a spare cage, or, if tame, can be given the run of the room. Water for drinking and/or bathing should

R. G. SPRACKLAND

Handling irascible monitors takes a fairly firm and steady hand, but should be practiced nevertheless, in the hopes that any monitors with bad tempers will learn to calm down and trust their keepers. Species shown is a Savannah Monitor, *Varanus exanthematicus*.

the whole cage should get a more thorough cleaning; materials should be removed and either discarded or scrubbed clean. The cage interior and its contents should be scrubbed with warm soapy water and a mild disinfectant such as household

be changed very regularly, preferably daily, or more often if necessary. The glass viewing panels should also be kept crystal clear, not only for the sake of hygiene, but because there is nothing worse-looking than a dirty, smeary, terrarium glass.

R. G. SPRACKLAND

Thanks to the efforts of so many top-notch monitor keepers, the hobby of herpetoculture has seen some fascinating moments. This young Green Tree Monitor, *Varanus prasinus*, for example, was the first of its species ever to be born in captivity (although sadly, it did not live long).

BREEDING SAVANNAH MONITORS

Every keeper of captive reptiles, including Savannah Monitors, should make every effort to encourage the animals to breed. Although monitors cannot be described as easy subjects to breed, successes seem to be on successful monitor breeding. Stimuli can include keeping sexes separate and introducing them at certain times (especially after a period of reduced temperature and/or photoperiod), or introducing a new male to an

G. DINGERKUS

Juvenile monitors are undeniably "cute," even for reptiles! The very distinct spotting on this Savannah Monitor, *Varanus exanthematicus*, is obviously very attractive, but will fade in time. At this age, such monitors can be fed lots of large insects.

the increase, though we have a fair distance to go before we can say we are breeding enough to meet demand in the pet industry. The ideal situation will arise when sufficient numbers are maintained so that it will be no longer necessary to import wild-caught specimens. This, of course, will also discourage the trade in smuggled reptiles.

As yet, there seems to be no positive strategy toward existing pair. By keeping two adult pairs and introducing them when a breeding response is required, it is likely that you will end up with both females gravid. Single pairs kept alone will often go for years with no attempt at breeding—perhaps never at all!

Male monitors are extremely territorial in their natural habitats, taking up an area of land with good cover and often a resident female or two, and

R. D. BARTLETT

Green Tree Monitors, *Varanus prasinus*, have continued to be captive-bred for some time, mainly due to their popularity with hobbyists. Considering how striking they are in appearance, this popularity is fairly understandable.

defending it vigorously against any intruding males. During such confrontations, the defending male curves his back and raises up his body by stretching his limbs to their full extent. At the same time the body and throat are inflated and the reptile emits loud hissing noises. Should the ground, the vanquished reptile will slowly retreat, though the victor will often apply simulated sexual activity. The process seems to be a trial of strength and courage rather than a serious fight and individuals are rarely injured.

By introducing two pairs

M. DUNBELBERGER

Stimulating monitors into mating is not a particularly painstaking affair. Here, two Dumeril's Monitors, *Varanus dumerili*, mate in a small plastic tub, which may appear somewhat cramped for them, but once monitors get going there aren't many distractions that can stop them.

threat fail to impress the intruder and cause him to submit (by crouching low), or retire, the intruder himself will take on a similar stance. Then, first circling each other warily, they eventually come to blows by pushing their bodies together from the sides, later by standing on the rear limbs and grappling while trying to force the opponent to the ground. Once forced to the together in the terrarium you can experience a similar ritual, but you should return the visiting pair back to their original accommodations before either male has submitted. This way you will have fooled both into thinking they have won and both will thus proceed to court and mate with their respective females.

Once a pair can get together without interference, courtship

R. D. BARTLETT

Below: The Bengal Monitor, *Varanus bengalensis*, was, at one time, a reasonably common species in the herpetoculturual hobby, but since it was placed on Appendix I of the CITES Endangered List it disappeared from collections and is not likely to return. It was not widely captive-bred when it was available. Photo by R. D. Bartlett.

Above: In many ways it is a shame that the Bengal Monitor, *Varanus bengalensis*, has become outlawed in the herpetocultural hobby. It is a remarkably pretty animal that reportedly adapted well to captive life, spending a great deal of time moving about rather than just sitting lethargically, and would take a wide variety of food items.

Above: Dumeril's Monitor, *Varanus dumerili*, has been bred through a number of generatations in captivity and, as you can tell by this photo, the juveniles are quite beautiful.

Facing page: If you have a female monitor that goes off her routine feeding schedule while gravid, do not be alarmed—this is normal and will reverse itself shortly after egglaying. Species shown is a Spiny-tail Monitor *Varanus acanthurus*.

begins. This consists of the male rubbing his head along the female's back and frequently nuzzling her neck and cloacal region. A receptive female will allow this procedure to take place without protest, but a non-receptive female will either retreat or take on an aggressive posture. Eventually the male moves his body partially across the female's back so that cloacas are side by side. Occasionally he will hold the female's neck in his mouth and hold her hind limbs back with his. He pushes her tail up with his tail, allowing him to twist the rear portion of his body under hers and he is then able to insert one of his hemipenes into her cloaca. Copulation usually takes place over a period of ten to 20 minutes while sperm is passed from the male into the female's receptacle. Copulation may take place several times over a period of days, the male often "camping" in a burrow close to that of the female so that she is more convenient; occasionally they will share the same burrow, but they usually emerge into the open in order to copulate. During the copulation the male may approach the female from either side, often using his hemipenes alternately. Should another male approach during copulation, the pair separate, the

R. D. BARTLETT

R. D. BARTLETT

The normal number of eggs in a monitor's clutch is around 20, give or take a few. Most monitors will appreciate a sandy substrate in which to dig their nests, and the deeper the better. Species shown is a Mangrove Monitor, *Varanus indicus*.

She will, however, drink water regularly. A gravid female will become noticeably plump as the eggs grow within her abdomen.

Suitable nesting sites often are scarce in the wild. These take into account the aspect of the sun, the ease with which the subsoil can be excavated, and the general safety of the area. In order to avoid wholesale egg predation by humans, domestic and wild animals, gravid females may travel long distances to find suitable sites. Termite mounds are often used in the wild, a burrow being excavated in the side of the mound facing the sun. Alternatively, nesting burrows are excavated directly into the ground, often into a slight slope facing the direction of the prevailing sun. Digging out the burrows with the front limbs, the rear limbs are used to push the excavated soil back. The length of the burrow is highly variable and may be up to 5 ft/1.5 m long, but the actual egg laying chamber is rarely more than 20 in/50 cm below the surface.

female taking refuge while the male drives off the intruder. After sexual activity diminishes the sexes again go their own separate ways to forage independently.

It takes about 50 to 70 days before fertilized eggs are ready to be laid. To a certain extent, egg development can be hastened or slowed depending on the conditions of temperature, humidity, food supply, and so on, so that they are ready to be laid at a favorable time. The female ceases to feed about four weeks before the eggs are due to be laid.

It often takes a day or more to excavate the nest, depending on the hardness of the ground or the termite mound. The latter are often very hard and excavation is very laborious for the lizard, which has to take frequent rests during the work. An enlarged chamber is excavated at the base of the burrow and when completed the female begins to lay her eggs. A normal clutch consists of 15 to 25 eggs, but 30 or more are not unusual. The record clutch of 46 eggs for the monitor

Above: Gillen's Pygmy Monitor, *Varanus gilleni*. **Below:** Savannah Monitor, *Varanus exanthematicus*.

species has been reported from the Savannah Monitor. After depositing the eggs, the female carefully fills in the burrow and then returns to her usual habitat. She may return to the vicinity of the nesting site for a few days after oviposition, but there is no

large enough enclosures you should provide them with a pit of moist sand about 3 ft/90 cm deep for natural egglaying. Captive female monitors are, however, often not satisfied with the egglaying facilities provided and will end up just spreading the

M. DUNKELBERGER

Female monitors are not known for showing any sort of parental care towards their eggs once they have been laid, so it is advisible that you take the eggs and incubate them artificially. Species shown is a Bengal Monitor, *Varanus bengalensis*.

evidence to suggest that she actually guards the nest against predators. Indeed, there seems to be no parental care once the eggs have been deposited, though there have been some unconfirmed suggestions that adults may return at hatching time to release hatchlings from the hard substrate.

If you keep your monitors in

eggs indiscriminately over the floor of the cage. Wherever the eggs are laid, they must be collected up for artificial incubation as facilities in the terrarium will be far too hit-and-miss for complete success. Those which are buried in a sandpit should be carefully dug out, while any laid on the cage floor (sometimes even in the water

R. D. BARTLETT

Monitor eggs can be incubated with a number of substrates, including soil, which was successfully used to produce these two Merten's Monitors, *Varanus mertensi*. Other subtrates include heavily granulated vermiculite and sphagnum moss.

bath) should be rescued as quickly as you can.

The leathery-shelled, white eggs are oval, each about 1.8 x 1.2 in/ 45 x 30 mm and weighing about 20 grams.

EGG INCUBATION

In the wild, the eggs rely on the sun-warmed substrate to provide the warmth for incubation. Captive-laid eggs, however, must be placed in an incubator. The soft shell is designed to absorb moisture from the substrate or incubation medium. Newly laid eggs often have dimples or collapsed areas, but these usually will soon fill out as moisture is absorbed. Keeping them up the same way as they were collected (mark the "top" with a non-toxic marker) they should be partially buried in an incubation medium contained in a shallow container. For convenience, the eggs can be laid in neat rows and buried to about three-quarters their thickness. The fourth quarter, left exposed, will allow you to inspect the eggs without disturbing them.

Many materials have been successfully used as incubation media (peat, sand, sawdust, paper towels, cotton towels, etc.) but, in my own experience, the most successful has been granular vermiculite. This is an inert, sterile, absorbent material, which is normally used in the horticultural industry or for insulation. It can be obtained in various grades, but a fine grade is best for general incubation purposes. A very absorbent material, vermiculite should be mixed with about its own weight of water before being placed in an incubation box. The lid of the incubation box should be provided with a few ventilation holes to allow for air circulation but, at the same time, help to conserve moisture. The box is placed in an incubator and maintained at around 81 to 95°F/ 27 to 35°C.

The type of incubator used seems to be unimportant as long as the correct temperature range can be provided. You can purchase an incubator, but since these are often rather expensive you may elect to make your own. A perfectly satisfactory incubator can, in fact, be made with an old fish tank or a simple wooden box containing an incandescent light bulb and a thermostat to regulate the temperature. With a thermometer in the box you will be able to experiment until you are sure that the correct temperatures are being maintained. It is best to use a red or blue bulb, or to mount the bulb in some sort of cover to minimize light intensity. Alternatively, a heat pad, a cable, or a porcelain heater may be used. By placing a dish of water in the incubator and warming it with an aquarium heater you will be able to increase heat and supplement the humidity.

The eggs will absorb moisture from the surrounding medium and increase in weight as the embryos develop. Infertile eggs do not absorb water, but do not be in a hurry to discard any eggs

ISABELLE FRANCAIS, COURTESY OF EUGENE L. BESSETTE

If you can afford the expense, it is advisable to acquire some commercial incubation apparatus, because, truthfully, the results are almost always very satisfying.

Many professional reptile breeders wholly rely on commercial incubators for all their incubation needs. When you're breeding thosands and thousands of dollars' worth of saleable stock, there can be no room for error.

G. DINGERKUS

Properly rearing varanid hatchlings involves many things, including frequent handling. This Nile Monitor, *Varanus niloticus*, for example, is a particularly tempermental animal if not handled, but it can be tamed with time and patience on the keeper's part.

unless you are quite sure they are spoiled.

The period of incubation can vary from about 140 to 180 days, often depending on the temperature and humidity. This incubation time can be frustrating, especially for beginners; you may even be tempted to open an egg up to see if the embryo is really developing. This won't prove anything except that the egg you chose was either developing or not. It may have been the only viable egg in the clutch! Patience is certainly a virtue here, however, and will hopefully be eventually rewarded with a batch of lively little monitors!

When ready to hatch, baby monitors slit open the tough, leathery eggshell with the egg tooth, a sharp projection on the snout which is shed shortly after hatching. Hatchlings are about 7 in/18 cm long and weigh about 20 grams. They are strongly patterned and brightly marked, compared with the duller appearance of adults. Once hatching has begun, the babies may seem to be taking a long time to free themselves from the shell, often 24 hours or more, but the temptation to "help" them is usually best avoided unless the reptile is having obvious difficulties. Occasionally the hatchling will stick tightly to the eggshell as a result of the fluids hardening by drying out too quickly. This can usually be avoided if the humidity is kept high; a gentle mist-spraying with lukewarm water may help. If the hatchling still sticks, you may have to resort to gently dabbing the affected parts with a piece of wadding soaked in lukewarm water until the reptile is freed.

REARING THE HATCHLINGS

Having completely left the eggshell and become free-moving, the hatchlings should be taken from the incubator and placed in "nursery" accommodations. Small glass or plastic aquarium tanks with ventilated lids are ideal; these may be kept in a larger heated terrarium or heated separately on heat tapes or pads. Moderate humidity should be maintained by having a shallow water-bath in each tank and by mist-spraying with lukewarm water every day, but do not keep the hatchlings permanently wet. It is essential that the baby monitors should have regular access to unfiltered direct sunlight or to broad-spectrum lighting as discussed earlier in the text. Do not attempt to remove the yolk sac from the babies since, once the contents have been absorbed, this will soon shrivel up, leaving a tiny scar on the underside.

With optimum conditions and a satisfactory diet, hatchling Savannah Monitors will hopefully start to feed within seven days (prior to this they will still be living on the contents of the yolk sac). They can be fed on crickets, grasshoppers, and mealworms, with the occasional pinkie mouse. A vitamin/mineral powder should be sprinkled on feed insects about twice per week.

Should certain kinds of food be ignored, keep trying others until you arrive at a satisfactory feeding regime. Once a youngster starts taking one kind of food, it will not be long before it is prepared to try others. Variety is the key to good health, so do not allow your monitors to overindulge in certain foods, otherwise they may grow too fast, become obese, will be useless for breeding, and may die prematurely. It is a good idea to weigh your specimens regularly and watch their growth progress. In any case, it is wise to keep records of the complete progress of your reptiles, both for your own use and that of others in the future. As your lizards grow, you can gradually introduce larger food items to the diet such as half grown mice or rats, day old chicks and so on. Lean meat and egg sprinkled with multivitamins should be given no more than once per week.

LONGEVITY

Little is known about the longevity of wild specimens. In captivity hatchlings can increase in weight up to four times in three months. They become sexually mature at three to four years, when they are approaching maximum adult size. Growth generally slows in the third year but never completely stops throughout life. Among the monitors, the Savannah Monitor holds the record of 17 or more years for captive longevity, though most specimens rarely live beyond 12 years.

Although the average keeper should never consider himself or herself to be any kind of "junior veterinarian," they can still acquire a few commercial products designed to help keep monitors in good health. One facet of reptile medical care that all keepers can and should practice is preventive medicine.

A VETERINARY PERSPECTIVE

All reptiles are remarkably resistant to diseases and most cases of ill-health among captive stock may usually be blamed on some inadequacy in their care. In recent research good progress has been made into the diagnosis and treatment of reptile diseases and many hitherto "hopeless" cases can now be successfully cured. Many veterinarians are now concerning themselves with the treatment of the more exotic kinds of pets, including monitors; some veterinary colleges are even including such data in their curricula. If your local veterinarian is not sure about a particular case, he or she should be able to communicate with one or more experts. Monitor keepers should not try other than the simplest of home treatments on their valuable pets but should use the services of a veterinarian whenever possible.

Some of the more usual conditions that may occur are as follows:

Bacterial Diseases: While there are many bacteria that are harmless or even beneficial to normal body functions, other forms are pathogenic. Monitors kept in unhygienic conditions are especially susceptible and the importance of scrupulous cleanliness cannot be over-emphasized. Most bacterial infections respond well to antibiotic or other treatment if caught in the early stages of infection. Consult your veterinarian.

Salmonellosis: Salmonella poisoning is known to have been transmitted from reptiles to man (especially from freshwater turtles; many *Salmonella* species have also been isolated from the feces of various lizards, and the possibility of it occurring in monitors cannot be ruled out). It is therefore important to thoroughly wash the hands after each cleaning or handling session. Salmonellosis manifests itself in unhealthy, watery, green-colored, foul-odored feces. If caught in its earlier stages, antibiotic treatment carried out by your veterinarian may be successful.

Protozoa: These microscopic, but relatively large, amoeba-like organisms cause infections of the gut. *Entamoeba invadens* is a fairly common protozoan infection which, if untreated, will rapidly reach epidemic proportions in captive monitors. Symptoms include watery, slimy feces, and general debility. Appropriate antibiotic treatment will be prescribed by your veterinarian.

Respiratory Infections: These may occasionally manifest themselves in stressed specimens. The patient will have difficulty in breathing, the nostrils will be blocked, and there will be a nasal discharge. Often the symptoms can be alleviated by moving the

K. H. SWITAK

Ticks are a common problem with monitors, especially those specimens that have recently been imported. However, ticks are not only easy to remove (in most cases), but they are also easy to spot in the first place. Any newly acquired monitors should be carefully inspected for ticks.

accidentally damaged for one reason or another. Skin infections should be referred to a veterinarian, who will give antimycotic, antiseptic, or antibiotic treatment, as appropriate. Deep infections and severe abscesses may be surgically opened, swabbed out, and then sutured, followed by a course of the appropriate medicines to prevent reinfection. Dysecdysis, the inability to shed properly, often as a result of a mite infestation or stress brought about by various other factors, may cause skin problems in monitors. Mite infestations should be cleared immediately (see below) and aid should be given to lizards experiencing difficulty in sloughing. Healthy monitors will slough (molt) their skins, problem-free, several times per year; a natural phenomenon related to growth. The skin is normally shed in patches and the whole process should take no more than a few days. Disease organisms can grow behind persistent patches of old skin which do not come off readily. The skin can often be loosened and peeled off by placing the reptile, for an hour or so, in a bath of very shallow, warm water.

patient to warmer, drier, well-ventilated quarters. In severe cases your veterinarian will recommend the appropriate treatment.

Skin Problems: There is a whole host of infections of the body surface which can be caused by fungi, bacteria, and viruses. Abscesses, which appear as lumps below the skin, are usually caused by infection building up in the flesh after the skin has been

Ticks and Mites: These are the most usual external parasites (ectoparasites) associated with monitors. Ticks are often found attached to newly captured specimens and may range up to ¼ in/6 mm in length. They fasten themselves with their piercing mouthparts to the lizard's skin, usually in a secluded spot between the scales, especially near the vent, or where the limbs join the body. Never attempt to pull a tick directly out, as its head may be left embedded in the skin, causing infection later. The tick's body should first be dabbed with a little alcohol (surgical spirit, meths, or even a drop of rum) to relax the mouthparts. The tick can then be gently twisted out with thumb and forefinger or with forceps.

Much smaller than ticks, mites often multiply to large numbers in indoor cages before they are even noticed. A large mite infestation can cause dysecdysis, stress, loss of appetite, anemia, and eventual death. Mites are also capable of transmitting blood diseases from one reptile to another. The reptile mite is smaller than a pinhead, has a round body, and is grayish in color, though it will be red if it has recently sucked blood. Mites may be seen running over the surfaces in an infected cage, particularly when you switch the lights on early in the morning, and their tiny, silvery, powdery droppings may be seen on the monitor's skin. Mites are most often introduced to the terrarium with new stock (another good reason for quarantine and careful inspection).

Fortunately, mites can be controlled quite easily by using a proprietary plastic insecticidal strip (of the type used to control houseflies). A small piece of such a strip placed in a perforated container and suspended in a terrarium will kill the mites in two to three days after which the strip is removed. As the strip does not kill mite eggs, the operation should be repeated ten days later to kill off any newly hatched mites. Two or three treatments will usually destroy all mites in the terrarium. It would be advisable also to spray the general areas around the terrarium with a surface spray insecticide, but do not use such a spray inside the terrarium as it could harm the reptiles.

Worm Infections: The internal parasites with which we are mainly concerned are various species of worm that live in the alimentary canal and feed on the monitor's partly digested food. In healthy lizards, worm numbers self-regulate and do not normally create major problems. In stressed or sick reptiles, however, the worms will proliferate in number, or grow larger, taking more of the lizard's food. The toxic waste materials of large numbers of worms may be an additional problem. Worms are therefore undesirable in captive monitors as they can cause complications, anemia and even death. By sending regular fecal samples from your monitors to a veterinary laboratory, you will have any worm infestations diagnosed. Various proprietary vermicides are available and your vet will be able to advise you of those specially suited for Savannah Monitors. Some of these may be given via the food but in severe cases you may have to get your vet to administer the medicine via stomach tube.

Wounds and Injuries: These may be caused by a monitor's attempting to escape (especially with regard to rubbing the snout raw along the terrarium glass or mesh—this is common in newly captured wild specimens), lamp burns, fighting, etc., and are susceptible to infection. All open wounds should be treated. Shallow wounds will usually heal automatically if swabbed daily with a mild antiseptic such as povidone-iodine. Deeper or badly infected wounds should be treated by a veterinarian as in some cases surgery and suturing may be required. Bone fractures, particularly in the limbs, may require some form of splinting in order to prevent malformation of the bone during healing. Again, your veterinarian should be consulted.

Nutritional Problems: These usually occur as a result of a lack of certain minerals or vitamins in the diet and are likely to affect monitors fed on a monotonous diet of, say, mealworms or raw meat. It is essential for monitors to have access to a variety of food items plus regular vitamin/ mineral supplements and an opportunity to bask in sunlight or artificial sunlight (full-spectrum lighting or similar). The incidence of disease will thus be dramatically minimized.

If one of your monitors dies and you don't know why, don't dispose of the corpse; save it and have someone do an autopsy on it as soon as possible. The reason for the death may effect your other monitors as well, so it is best to know what occurred. Species shown is an Argus Monitor, *Varanus panoptes*.

R. G. SPRACKLAND

SUGGESTED READING

PS-311, 96 pgs, 60+ photos · SK-015, 64 pgs. 40+ photos

PS-316, 128 pgs, 100+ photos · KW-196, 128 pgs, 100+ photos · PS-769, 192 pgs, 120+ photos

TU-025, 64 pgs, 60+ photos · SK-032, 64 pgs, 40+ photso · YF-111, 32 pgs

TS-145, 288 pgs, 250+ photos

t.f.h.

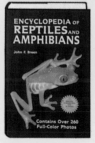

KW-197, 128 pgs, 110+ photos · H-935, 576 pgs, 260+ photos

TS-166, 192 pgs, 170+ photos

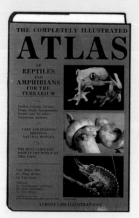

H-1102, 830 pgs, 1800+ Illus and photos · TS-165, 655 pgs, (2 vol.) 1800+ photos